MW01643988

Flawless Love

Divine Messages from a Wretched Man in Love with Jesus

Nic Sigala

Second printing, 2025

Published by Gospel of Growth, Maysville, MO 64469

www.GospelofGrowth.com

My soul delights in the scriptures, and my heart ponders them, and I write them for the learning and the profit of my children. Behold, my soul delights in the things of the Lord; and my heart ponders continually upon the things which I have seen and heard... my heart exclaims: O wretched man that I am! Yes, my heart sorrows because of my flesh.

Awake, my soul! No longer droop in sin. Rejoice, O my heart, and give place no more for the enemy of my soul... Rejoice, O my heart, and cry unto the Lord, and say: O Lord, I will praise thee forever; yea, my soul will rejoice in thee, my God, and the rock of my salvation.

~ Nephi

DEDICATION

This book is for Jesus Christ—the One who flipped my life upside down and showed me what real love is. Every word here, every story, every struggle, every victory—it's all for His glory. I wouldn't be who I am today without Him. He's the reason I'm still standing.

To my wife Mistie: You're a walking example of God's grace in my life. Thank you for your love, your strength, and for standing beside me through the chaos. God's not done showing His goodness through you.

To my kids: Listen to me—you have a purpose. God made you for greatness, and I pray you'll lean into Him and never let go. He's got you. Always.

To you—the reader: You're here for a reason. Whether you feel broken, lost, or on top of the world, know this—Jesus Christ sees you, He loves you, and He's waiting for you. Don't miss this opportunity to let Him change your life.

TABLE OF CONTENTS

PREFACE: MY JOURNEY INTO FLAWLESS LOVE 1

SECTION 1: FOUNDATIONS OF FAITH 3

CHAPTER 1: A JOURNEY FROM DARKNESS TO LIGHT 5
CHAPTER 2: EMBRACING UNCONDITIONAL LOVE 9
CHAPTER 3: BE STILL & KNOW 13
CHAPTER 4: HE FIGHTS OUR BATTLES 17

SECTION 2: WALKING WITH CHRIST 23

CHAPTER 5: LETTING GO 25
CHAPTER 6: FAITH TO BE HEALED 31
CHAPTER 7: THE DIVINE PROMISES OF JOHN 14 37
CHAPTER 8: SPIRITUAL WARFARE 41
CHAPTER 9: EMBERS OF ENDURANCE 47
CHAPTER 10: BEAUTY BIRTHED FROM CHAOS 53
CHAPTER 11: IRREVOCABLE BLESSINGS 59

SECTION 3: LIVING IN FLAWLESS LOVE 65

CHAPTER 12: THE ESSENCE OF LOVE 67
CHAPTER 13: THE POWER OF GRATITUDE AND LOVE 73
CONCLUSION: THE CALL TO FOLLOW HIM 79
EPILOGUE: FLAWLESS LOVE IN A FLAWED WORLD 85

PREFACE

MY JOURNEY INTO FLAWLESS LOVE

Let me be real with you—this book isn't about me. It's about Jesus and how He transformed my life when I thought I was too far gone. I'm not here to impress you or sugarcoat anything. My story is messy, raw, and full of mistakes, but it's proof that God can take anyone—even a guy like me—and turn their life into something beautiful.

Back in 2021, everything changed. I was minding my business, just trying to survive another day, and then BOOM—the Lord hit me with a vision. He asked me to follow Him into the wilderness. Not metaphorically. Literally. He called me out of everything I knew and told me to bring His message to the people who've been forgotten—the ones the world writes off. I couldn't say no.

But here's the thing no one tells you: walking with Jesus will cost you everything. My reputation? Gone. My business? Done. My freedom? Taken, even if only for a time. But let me tell you something—knowing Him, serving Him, and seeing Him work miracles in the lives of others? Worth. Every. Single. Thing.

I've been through hell and back. I've had my name dragged through the mud, lost almost everything, and faced situations that would break most people. But I'm still here because God is real, and

His love is flawless. I've seen Him show up time and time again—like when He saved me from people who wanted me gone or gave me strength when I thought I had none. He's a promise-keeper, and He's never let me down.

This book is my testimony. I'm not writing this as some perfect dude with a polished life. I'm just a guy who's been wrecked by God's love and wants to tell the world about it. If you take anything away from these pages, let it be this: Jesus loves you, and He's got a plan for you that's bigger than your wildest dreams. I'm proof of that.

So, buckle up. This is a journey of redemption, healing, and hope. I'm here to tell you that no matter where you've been, no matter what you've done, God's not done with you. Let's go.

SECTION 1

FOUNDATIONS OF FAITH

CHAPTER 1

A JOURNEY FROM DARKNESS TO LIGHT

Let me take you back to the beginning. Life didn't hand me a guidebook or a smooth path. I grew up in chaos—real, gut-wrenching chaos. By the time I was 11, my parents were gone. Drugs, trauma, and darkness disconnected them from me, and I was left to fend for myself. It's hard to explain what it feels like to be a kid, looking at the people who are supposed to love and protect you, and realizing they're not going to be there for you. It shatters something deep inside you.

From there, it was one bad situation after another—foster homes, shelters, juvenile detention centers. I became a number in the system, a name on a list, a problem no one wanted to deal with. I learned to survive, but survival comes at a cost. You shut down. You stop trusting. You start to believe the lie that you're unlovable, unwanted, and unworthy. And you carry that with you everywhere you go.

By 15, I was living that lie to the fullest. I got mixed up in gang life, running with guys who were just as broken as I was. We stole cars, robbed people, and acted like we were untouchable. But the truth is, I was scared. I was angry. I didn't know how else to cope. Then one night, everything came crashing down. We got caught.

I'll never forget sitting in that jail cell, staring at the cold, gray walls. I was facing 20 years behind bars. Twenty years. For a 15-year-old kid, that's a death sentence. I felt like my life was over. For the first time, I didn't know how to fight or run or survive. All I could do was sit there in the stillness and cry out to a God I wasn't even sure existed.

"God, if You're real, help me. I can't do this. I don't know what to do. Are you really there?"

That's all I had—a desperate, broken prayer. And do you know what? God answered. Not with thunder or lightning or some miraculous jailbreak. He moved through people. My aunt and uncle—people I barely knew—walked into that courtroom and told the judge, "We'll take him in. We'll be responsible for him."

I couldn't believe it. I was a mess, a criminal, a kid who'd made nothing but bad choices, and here they were, offering me a second chance. The judge sentenced me to 16 weeks at Thunderbird Youth Academy, a boot camp for troubled kids. It wasn't easy—trust me, they worked us hard—but it saved my life.

When I got out, my aunt and uncle took me into their home. For the first time, I had a comfortable bed, a family, and a sense of stability. Their house wasn't just a shelter—it was a sanctuary. They didn't preach at me or force religion down my throat. They showed me love, patience, and grace and taught me the gospel through example. They introduced me to Jesus, and at 15, I got baptized.

I'd love to tell you that everything changed after that—that I became a new person overnight. But the truth? I wasn't ready to let go of my old life. Survival mode was still my default. I brought chaos into their peaceful home—lying, rebelling, and breaking their trust. They loved me anyway. But I wasn't ready to change.

The years that followed were a blur of bad decisions. I got married too young, messed that up, and tried again with another marriage that fell apart just as quickly. Addiction sank its claws into me—methamphetamines, opiates, anything to numb the pain. I was spiraling, but I didn't know how to stop. Then, at 30, the unthinkable happened.

My brother Jimmy was murdered. Shot during a drug deal gone wrong. That news hit me like a freight train. I was angry—at the people who killed him, at myself for not being there, and at God for letting it happen. I wanted revenge. I wanted to make them pay. But in the middle of my rage, something happened that I'll never forget.

God spoke to me.

It wasn't a feeling or a whisper. It was His voice, clear and undeniable. He said, "Nic, who do you think you are to deserve my grace more than they do? **I am NO respecter of persons** and have never looked at sin with the least degree of variance...and you all fall short. You need to forgive them. My grace is sufficient for them too."

Forgive them? The people who took my brother from me? No way. I fought it. I wrestled with God, telling Him why they didn't deserve grace. But He wouldn't let up. Day after day, He pressed on my heart until I finally broke. I was sitting in my car one night, screaming at the sky, and then I just let go. "Okay, God. I'll forgive them. But You're gonna have to help me because I can't do it on my own."

And He did. That moment of surrender changed everything. Forgiving them didn't mean what they did was okay, but it set me free. It opened the door for God to start working in my heart, healing the wounds I'd carried for so long.

Over time, I began to see my life through a different lens. I saw how God had been with me in every moment, even when I didn't realize it. He was there in that jail cell when I cried out to Him. He was there in my aunt and uncle's love. He was there when I was drowning in addiction, waiting for me to reach for His hand. And He was there in my brother's death, turning my grief into a catalyst for change.

Here's what I want you to know: It doesn't matter how far you've fallen or how broken you feel. God's love is relentless. His grace is for everyone—the lost, the hurting, the angry, the ones who think they're beyond saving. I'm living proof of that. If He can take a messed-up kid like me and turn my life around, He can do the same for you. I testify to you in the name of Jesus Christ that He is NO respecter of persons and He loves you. Nothing can separate you form His love. Nothing.

REFLECTION PROMPT:

- Think about a time in your life when you felt broken or lost. How might God have been working behind the scenes, even if you didn't see it at the time?

____

____

____

____

____

____

____

____

____

____

____

____

CHAPTER 2

EMBRACING UNCONDITIONAL LOVE

Forgiveness isn't a one-time decision. It's a process—a battle between holding onto your pain and trusting God to heal it. And let me tell you, it's not easy. When my brother Jimmy was murdered, I wanted justice. No, scratch that—I wanted revenge. I wanted the people who took his life to feel the weight of my grief, to suffer the way I was suffering.

God had other plans.

I told you how God spoke to me after Jimmy's death, how He whispered, *"You need to forgive them. My grace is sufficient for them too."* But what I didn't tell you is how hard that was to accept. At first, I thought, *Okay, fine. I forgive them.* But if I'm being honest, it was just words. Deep down, I wasn't ready to let go of the pain. Holding onto it felt like a way to honor Jimmy, to validate my suffering. It felt safer than opening my heart to the vulnerability of forgiveness.

For months, I wrestled with God. Every time I prayed, He reminded me of His love—His love for me, for Jimmy, and yes, even for Enrique and Laquinta, the people responsible for my brother's death. I'd hear His voice, gentle but persistent: *"Trust Me. Let Me show you the depths of My love."*

I wanted to trust Him, but it was a struggle. Forgiveness felt like letting them off the hook, like saying what they did was okay.

But God kept showing me that forgiveness wasn't about them—it was about me. It was about releasing the chains of bitterness that were keeping me from fully experiencing His love.

Nine months later, I found myself in a courtroom, facing the very people I thought I'd never be able to forgive. The trial was brutal—reliving the pain, hearing the details of what happened to Jimmy. My family was invited to speak, and I knew I had to take the stand.

I stood there, looking Enrique and Laquinta in the eyes, and I felt this overwhelming sense of peace. It wasn't my peace—it was God's. And in that moment, I finally understood what forgiveness really meant. It wasn't about excusing their actions. It was about acknowledging God's love for them, even in the midst of their sin, and trusting Him to deal with their hearts.

I took a deep breath and said, "I want you to know that God loves you. You are forgiven—not because of anything you've done, but because of His grace. Now it's time for you to learn to accept the consequences of your actions and forgive yourselves. You have a hard road ahead of you and I want you to know that God will be with you. Every. Step. Of. The. Way."

The courtroom was silent. I could see the weight of my words sinking in. It wasn't about me anymore—it was about God using my brokenness to bring His light into a dark place.

Enrique is still serving his life sentence. I pray for him often, asking God to meet him in that prison cell and show him the same love and grace that saved me. But Laquinta? She got out in 2022, and what happened next still amazes me.

I ran into her by chance. At first, it was awkward—what do you even say to someone who took part in your brother's death? But then she started talking, and I could see the change in her. I invited her to consider God's love for her and used my forgiveness for her as an example of that eternal love and then I asked her If she would begin having a relationship with the Savior. I reminded her of what I'd said in the courtroom: "God loves you, and you're forgiven." She smiled through tears and said, "I know. I believe it."

That moment was a full-circle miracle. It reminded me that God's love isn't just for the innocent or the righteous—it's for the broken, the lost, the ones who think they're too far gone. It's for *everyone*.

The Bible says, *"For I am convinced that neither death nor life, neither angels nor demons, neither the present nor the future, nor any powers, neither height nor depth, nor anything else in all creation, will be able to separate us from the love of God that is in Christ Jesus our Lord"* (Romans 8:38–39). That love is unshakable, unbreakable, and completely undeserved. It's what allowed me to forgive, and it's what gave Laquinta a second chance.

Here's what I want you to know: Forgiveness is hard. It might take months, years, or even a lifetime. But it starts with a choice—a choice to trust God and let His love work through you. You don't have to figure it out all at once. Just take the first step, and let Him lead you the rest of the way.

When you embrace God's unconditional love, it changes everything. It heals wounds you thought would never close. It frees you from the prison of bitterness. And it gives you the strength to see others—not as their worst mistakes, but as children of God, loved and cherished just like you.

If God's love can transform me—and Laquinta—it can transform you too. Don't wait. Open your heart, and let Him in.

Reflection Prompt:

1. Is there someone in your life you're struggling to forgive? Ask God to show you His love for them—and for you.
2. Take a moment to thank God for His unconditional love. Write down how that love has impacted your life.

CHAPTER 3

BE STILL & KNOW

There's a lot of noise in this world. Noise from the outside—people's opinions, threats, accusations—and noise from the inside—our fears, doubts, and anxieties. It's relentless, and if we're not careful, it can consume us. But in the middle of the storm, God whispers: *"Be still, and know that I am God"* (Psalm 46:10).

That verse—simple as it is—has been a lifeline for me. It's not just words on a page; it's a practice, a promise, and a way of living. I learned that the hard way during one of the darkest seasons of my life.

When I got out of jail in 2021, I wasn't stepping into freedom. It felt like I was stepping into another prison—a prison of fear, loss, and hatred. People were trying to kill me. No exaggeration. The false accusations against me had stirred up so much anger that it felt like the world was against me. My farm was burned to the ground. I was stalked, harassed, and threatened. Every day, I woke up not knowing if I'd make it to the end of the day. To make matters worse, my family had been stripped from me, and I was left with nothing but the ashes of what my life used to be.

If there was ever a time to panic, that was it. Most people would've been drowning in fear or consumed by rage. And trust me, I felt both of those things. But instead of letting them control me, I turned to God. Not because I'm some kind of saint, but because I'd learned—through years of trial and error—that stillness is the only way to survive the storm.

Stillness didn't come naturally to me. It was a skill I had to develop, a discipline I had to practice over and over until it became my default response. For me, it started with something simple: breathing. When I felt the panic rising—my heart pounding, my chest tightening, my thoughts spinning out of control—I'd stop and focus on my breath. Slow, deep breaths. In through my nose, out through my mouth. Over and over, until my body started to calm down.

At first, it felt almost mechanical. Like I was just going through the motions. But as I practiced, I started to notice something amazing. The more I breathed, the more I became aware of God's presence. It was like He was waiting for me in that stillness, ready to meet me as soon as I slowed down enough to notice Him.

There were nights when the threats and harassment felt unbearable. I'd sit in the dark, breathing, praying, and crying out to God. "Lord, I don't know how much more of this I can take. I need You." And every single time, He showed up. Not in some dramatic way—no lightning bolts or angelic choirs. Just His quiet, steady presence, like a warm blanket wrapping around me. His peace didn't make the problems disappear, but it gave me the strength to face them.

One night, I remember sitting in my truck after yet another round of threats. My farm was gone. My family was gone. My reputation was in tatters. I felt like everything I'd ever worked for had been ripped away. But as I sat there, focusing on my breathing and praying, I felt God's whisper in my heart: *"I'm here. I've got you. Be still."*

That was the moment I realized something profound: Stillness isn't about doing nothing. It's not about ignoring the problems or pretending everything's fine. It's about actively surrendering to God. It's about saying, *"I can't handle this, Lord, but I know You can."* And that surrender? It's the most freeing thing in the world.

The Bible is full of stories about the power of stillness. Think about Moses at the Red Sea. Pharaoh's army was closing in behind them, and the Israelites were panicking. But Moses said, *"The Lord will fight for you; you need only to be still"* (Exodus 14:14). Or Elijah, hiding in a cave after running for his life. He didn't hear God in the wind, the earthquake, or the fire—it was in the gentle whisper that God revealed Himself (1 Kings 19:12).

Stillness isn't weakness. It's strength. It's the courage to stop striving and let God take over. It's the trust to believe that He's working, even when we can't see it.

Through stillness, I endured things that should've broken me. The threats, the lies, the harassment—they didn't define me. God's presence did. His love carried me through every moment of that storm, and it's the only reason I'm still standing today.

Let me be clear: Stillness doesn't mean passivity. It doesn't mean you sit back and do nothing while life falls apart. It means you root yourself in God's presence so that when you do act, you're acting from a place of peace and clarity, not fear and chaos. It means you let Him guide your steps instead of rushing ahead on your own.

I don't know what storm you're facing right now. Maybe it's fear. Maybe it's grief. Maybe it's anger that feels like it's eating you alive. Whatever it is, I want you to know this: God is with you. His peace is available to you. But you have to make space for it. You have to slow down, breathe, and let Him in.

Stillness saved me. It didn't fix everything overnight, but it gave me the strength to keep going. It gave me the perspective to see God's hand at work, even in the darkest moments. And it reminded me, over and over, that I'm never alone.

You're not alone either. Take a breath. Sit in His presence. Let Him carry you. He's bigger than the storm, and He's already fighting for you.

Reflection Prompt:

1. What noise in your life is drowning out God's voice? How can you create space for stillness this week?
2. Take five minutes today to sit quietly with God. Focus on your breathing, invite Him into your space, and listen for His whisper.
3. Write down any thoughts, feelings, or impressions you experience during this time of stillness.

CHAPTER 4

HE FIGHTS OUR BATTLES

There is nothing—*nothing*—in this life more powerful than the name of Jesus. Not fear, not darkness, not death itself. His name has the power to shift the atmosphere, to break chains, and to silence the forces of hell. I'm not just saying this because it sounds good. I'm saying it because I've lived it. I've seen it with my own eyes. I've felt it in my own life. And let me tell you—when you're standing in the middle of chaos, surrounded by enemies, and you call on His name? Everything changes.

THE FIGHT THAT NEVER HAPPENED

It was 2021. My life was already a wreck. The false accusations, the stalking, the harassment—it felt like the world was out to destroy me. I had been stripped of my family, my reputation, and almost everything I had built. I was in survival mode, leaning on the Lord for every step. But even in the midst of all that, God was teaching me something profound about His power, His presence, and the authority we have as His followers.

One night, I went out to dinner with a friend. Let's call him Frankie. Now, Frankie was a force of nature. A former cage fighter, he was a giant of a man with a temper to match. He had a good heart, but when alcohol was in the mix, all bets were off. Frankie became unpredictable, explosive, and downright dangerous. That night, he wanted to go to a local dive bar to shoot pool. I agreed, thinking it would be harmless fun. I had no idea what we were walking into.

When we arrived, the place was packed. There was a country band playing, people were drinking and dancing, and the energy in the room was... off. You could feel it—a heaviness, a tension in the air. As we made our way to the pool tables, Frankie noticed a group of about ten guys surrounding a much smaller man. They weren't just messing with him. They were bullying him, intimidating him, and it was clear they were gearing up to hurt him.

Now, Frankie wasn't the kind of guy to stand by and let something like that happen. He marched right over and stepped in. "Leave him alone," he said, his voice firm, his presence commanding. The problem was, these weren't strangers. Frankie had a history with some of these guys, and it wasn't good. The moment they saw him, the situation escalated. The smaller man slipped away, and now the group turned their attention to Frankie. Ten against one. Voices rose, fists clenched, and the room started to shift. People backed away, clearing space for what was about to go down.

I could see it unfolding in slow motion. Frankie, already buzzed from dinner, standing his ground. The other men, fueled by anger and alcohol, closing in. The tension was so thick you could feel it pressing on your chest. It was about to erupt, and there was nothing I could do to stop it.

But then I heard it. The Lord's voice, clear as day: *"Cast out the darkness and command peace in My name."*

Let me tell you, I didn't feel brave. I didn't feel strong. I felt like a guy standing in the middle of a bar about to witness his friend get torn apart. But when God speaks, you listen. I raised my right arm to the square, took a deep breath, and said, with every ounce of authority He had given me: "In the name of Jesus Christ, I command the darkness to depart. Be still."

The entire bar went silent.

The band stopped playing. Conversations died. It was like the air had been sucked out of the room. People told me later that my voice seemed to boom through the building, louder than the music, louder than the shouting. Some even said it looked like I grew taller, like the presence of God Himself was standing there with me. And maybe He was, because what happened next was nothing short of a miracle.

The tension dissolved. The fight that was moments away from erupting simply... stopped. The group of men backed off, one by one, their expressions shifting from anger to confusion. It was like someone had flipped a switch, draining the hostility out of the room. The band started playing again, and just like that, the storm was over.

As we were leaving, one of the men who had been ready to fight Frankie pulled me aside. "Hey man," he said, his voice low. "I don't know what just happened, or what came over me, but... thank you. Thank you for speaking His name."

That moment hit me like a freight train. I had always known there was power in Jesus' name, but that night, I *saw* it. I saw darkness flee. I saw peace take over. I saw hearts begin to change—not because of me, but because of Him. It was a reminder that no matter how overwhelming the battle feels, we serve a God who is bigger, stronger, and always fighting on our behalf.

The Reality of Spiritual Warfare

That night wasn't just about stopping a bar fight. It was about something much bigger. The Bible tells us, *"For our struggle is not against flesh and blood, but against the rulers, against the authorities, against the powers of this dark world and against the spiritual forces of evil in the heavenly realms"* (Ephesians 6:12).

What I witnessed wasn't just a physical confrontation—it was a spiritual one. Darkness had crept into that bar, feeding anger, division, and violence. But when the name of Jesus was spoken, the darkness had no choice but to flee. That's the reality of spiritual warfare. It's not something out of a movie. It's happening every day, in our homes, our communities, and our hearts. But the good news? We're not fighting alone.

Trusting God to Fight for You

God doesn't call us to fight every battle ourselves. In fact, He often calls us to step back and let Him take over. *"The Lord will fight for you; you need only to be still"* (Exodus 14:14). That doesn't mean we're passive. It means we stand firm in faith, trusting that He will do what only He can do.

I've seen this play out in my life more times than I can count. From the threats and harassment to the loss of my family to that night in the bar, God has shown up again and again, proving that He is faithful, powerful, and always present. His name has carried me through fires I thought would consume me. It's brought peace to situations that should've destroyed me. And it reminded me that no matter what I face, I'm never alone.

The Power of His Name

There is power in the name of Jesus. Power to heal, to protect, to break chains, and to cast out darkness. It's not just a name—it's a declaration of who He is. When we speak His name, we're calling on the King of kings, the Lord of lords, the One who has already defeated sin, death, and every force of evil.

Whatever battle you're facing right now, speak His name. Trust Him to fight for you. And watch as the darkness flees.

REFLECTION PROMPT:

1. What battles are you fighting today? Have you called on the name of Jesus to intervene?
2. Reflect on a time when you experienced the power of His name. How did it change the situation?
3. Pray this week, asking God to reveal His power in your life and to fight the battles you cannot.

SECTION 2

WALKING WITH CHRIST

CHAPTER 5

LETTING GO

Letting go is one of the hardest things you'll ever do. It goes against every instinct we have. We cling to what we love, hold tightly to our plans, and fight like crazy to make things turn out the way we want. But sometimes, God asks us to loosen our grip, to step back, and to trust Him with the very things we're most afraid to lose. That's where real faith begins—not in the holding on, but in the letting go.

For me, that lesson came at a time when everything I valued had already been ripped away. My family was gone. My reputation was in shreds. My life was a pile of ashes, and I was desperate to rebuild it. I prayed, I pleaded, I begged God for a way to fix it all. I thought if I could just say the right words or do the right thing, I could somehow get my family back, repair my marriage, and put my life back together. But no matter how hard I tried, nothing changed.

I'll never forget the night God confronted me. I was on my knees, praying like my life depended on it, pouring out my pain and my frustration. I told Him how much I missed my kids, how much I wanted to heal my relationship with my wife. I begged Him for strength, for answers, for some kind of hope. And then, in the middle of my desperation, I heard Him speak: *"Nic, you trust Me with you, but will you also trust Me with them?"*

I froze. That question cut straight to the heart of my struggle. I had been trusting God to carry me through my pain, but I hadn't trusted Him to care for my family. I still thought it was my job to fix everything, to make things right. But in that moment, I realized how tightly I had been holding on, how afraid I was to let go.

God was asking me to release them into His hands—to trust that He loved them even more than I did and that He could care for them better than I ever could. It was one of the hardest things He's ever asked me to do.

THE STRUGGLE TO LET GO

Surrender doesn't happen overnight. It's not a one-time decision—it's a battle. For weeks, I wrestled with God. Every time I thought I had let go, I'd catch myself trying to take control again, making plans, running through scenarios in my head. I wanted to trust Him, but part of me was still afraid. What if He didn't fix things? What if His plan wasn't what I wanted?

There's a song by For King and Country called "Control" that captures this struggle perfectly. The lyrics say:

> *"You asked me to let go, but I thought I knew better / Afraid of surrender and what I don't know... I give up control."*

That's exactly where I was. Afraid of surrender. Afraid of what would happen if I truly let go. But the more I prayed, the more God reminded me of who He is. He isn't just my Father—He's theirs too. He isn't just my Shepherd—He's the One who watches over all His children. Slowly, I began to loosen my grip, to release my plans, my expectations, and my fears into His hands.

It wasn't easy. I cried. I questioned. I had to bring the same struggle to God over and over again. But each time I surrendered, I felt a little more peace. I started to see that letting go wasn't about giving up—it was about giving over. It was about trusting that the God who created the universe could handle my family too.

The Breakthrough

The moment I truly let go, everything began to shift. Not because I did something, but because God was already working behind the scenes. A few months after that prayer, the criminal charges against me were dropped. The no-contact order was lifted. And out of nowhere, my kids came to stay with me. We went from having no contact to spending the majority of our time together.

No, my marriage wasn't restored the way I'd hoped, but God brought healing in other ways. My ex-wife and I were able to move forward in our roles as co-parents. The bitterness and pain that had defined our relationship began to ease. God didn't answer my prayers the way I expected, but He answered them in ways that were better than I could have imagined.

The Danger of Control

Here's what I learned through that experience: Control is a thief. It robs you of peace, joy, and clarity. When you're holding onto something so tightly, it's impossible to see what God is doing. You're too focused on your own plans, your own fears, your own strength. And when things don't go the way you expect, the frustration is unbearable.

I see this all the time—not just in my own life, but in the lives of the people around me. We create these expectations for how life should be, and when reality doesn't match up, we crumble. We get angry at God. We blame ourselves. We spiral into anxiety, trying to fix things that were never ours to fix in the first place.

But when you let go—when you release the weight of control and hand it over to God—everything changes. Surrender doesn't mean you stop caring. It doesn't mean you stop praying or stop hoping. It means you stop striving. It means you stop holding onto the illusion that you're in charge and trust the One who actually is.

Jesus said, *"Come to me, all you who are weary and burdened, and I will give you rest. Take my yoke upon you and learn from me, for I am gentle and humble in heart, and you will find rest for your souls. For my yoke is easy and my burden is light"* (Matthew 11:28–30).

That's the promise of surrender: rest. Peace. Freedom. When you let go of the burden of control, you make room for God to carry it for you. And trust me, His hands are big enough to hold it all.

THE FREEDOM OF SURRENDER

Looking back now, I see how God was working in every moment of that season. He didn't give me what I wanted, but He gave me what I needed. He taught me to trust Him—not just with my life, but with the people I love most. And in doing so, He brought a peace that no amount of control could ever produce.

Letting go doesn't mean you stop loving. It doesn't mean you stop fighting for what's right. It means you trust the One who holds all things together. It means you believe, with every fiber of your being, that His plan is better than yours.

Whatever you're holding onto today—your family, your future, your fears, your failures—release it. Trust Him. Let go of control and watch what He does. I promise you, His hands are strong enough to carry it.

REFLECTION PROMPT:

1. What are you holding onto that God is asking you to release? Why is it hard to let go?
2. Write a prayer of surrender, giving your fears, plans, or loved ones into God's hands. Reflect on how it feels to release control.

3. Read Matthew 11:28–30 and Proverbs 3:5–6. What do these verses reveal about God's heart for you?

CHAPTER 6

FAITH TO BE HEALED

Let's get one thing straight: God heals. No "maybe," no "sometimes," no "if you're lucky." He *heals*. Physically. Emotionally. Spiritually. That's who He is. The Healer. The Restorer. But here's the kicker—it takes faith. Not wishy-washy, *"I hope this works"* faith. Real, bold, *"I'm putting everything on the line because I believe You can do this"* faith. And when that kind of faith meets the power of Jesus Christ? Miracles happen. I've seen it.

HUBERT: LIFE RESTORED

Let me tell you about Hubert. The guy was 80 years old, full of love for his family, and one of the kindest people you'd ever meet. But his body? It was giving out. COVID had wrecked him, and he was in and out of the hospital so much that eventually, the doctors just gave up. Hospice set him up at home so he could die in peace. His family was heartbroken, but they called me and the Bishop to come and give him a priesthood blessing.

The Bishop pulls me aside before we go in and says, *"Nic, we need to prepare the family for Hubert's passing. Let's release him and help them let go."* Heavy stuff, right? We walk in, and Hubert's lying in a hospital bed in the living room. The guy looked like death.

Pale, thin, barely breathing. His family said he couldn't even speak without them leaning in real close to hear him.

I leaned down, and Hubert whispered, *"Brother Nic, I love you."* I kissed his forehead and said, *"Brother Hubert, I love you too."* And that's when it happened. The Lord pricked my heart and said, *"Nic, bless him with life and vitality."*

Now let me be real with you—this was bold. The Bishop was literally reading scriptures to prepare the family for Hubert's death. But when God speaks, you listen. I laid my hands on Hubert's head and prayed like I've never prayed before. I commanded life to come into his body in the name of Jesus Christ. I called on angels to stand with us. And I spoke healing, strength, and vitality into his body according to his faith.

When we finished, the Bishop gave me a look like I had lost my mind. But I knew I had done what God told me to do.

A few days later, I went back to check on the family. As I pulled up, a white pickup truck rolled in. Guess who was driving? Hubert. He jumped out of that truck, hugged me tight, and said, *"Brother Nic, I've been healed! Hallelujah!"* The guy who was supposed to die just days earlier was now walking, driving, and praising the Lord. That's the power of faith. Hubert had faith to be healed.

Charlotte: Healing That Defied Logic

Then there's Charlotte. She lived in the same house as Hubert and was struggling with a torn ACL. Surgery was already scheduled, but she wasn't ready to give up hope. She called me and asked for a blessing. I showed up with a homemade CBD salve I'd been working on for inflammation, laid my hands on her head, and prayed in Jesus' name.

"Charlotte," I said, "if you will exercise your faith in the Lord Jesus Christ, He will heal you. I command this to be so on His authority."

Fast forward three days. Charlotte goes in for her surgery, and the doctors run some pre-op scans. They stop. They're puzzled. Why? Because the tear in her ACL is gone. She didn't need surgery. The doctors couldn't explain it, but Charlotte could. She looked them in the eye and said, *"I had the faith to be healed, and the Lord healed me."* Simple as that.

Charlotte had faith to be healed.

SARA: FAITH IN ACTION

And then there's Sara. She was 27, one of my late brother Jimmy's best friends. By 2022, she was in kidney failure. Her body was weak, her future looked bleak, and she was running out of options. My wife Mistie—an angel the Lord sent into my life—and I felt impressed one day to drive around the neighborhood, ministering to whoever the Lord led us to. That's when we found Sara.

She was sitting in her home, tired, worn down, and hurting. We prayed with her, and I asked her, *"Sara, do you believe that Jesus Christ can heal you?"* She said yes. I said, *"Then let us lay our hands on you and bless you."* She agreed.

Mistie was the mouthpiece for the blessing, and she didn't hold back. She prayed with boldness, declaring healing and restoration in the name of Jesus Christ. She asked for His light and love to fill Sara's body and bring her back to health.

The next week, Sara went to her doctor. They ran some tests and said her kidneys were improving. At her next appointment, they were blown away—her kidneys were fully restored. No explanation. No medical reason. Just the undeniable power of God.

Sara had the faith to be healed.

Faith That Moves Mountains

Here's what I want you to take away from these stories: Faith isn't a backup plan. It's not your last resort. It's the key to unlocking the miraculous. The Bible says, *"Without faith, it is impossible to please God"* (Hebrews 11:6). And Jesus Himself said, *"If you have faith as small as a mustard seed, you can say to this mountain, 'Move from here to there,' and it will move. Nothing will be impossible for you"* (Matthew 17:20).

Faith isn't passive. It's active. It's bold. It's stepping out and trusting God to show up. Sometimes, that means miraculous healing. Other times, it means strength to endure. But every time, it means experiencing the power and presence of the living God.

Reflection Prompt

1. Is there an area of your life where you need healing? Bring it to God in faith.
2. Reflect on Mark 5:25–34. What does the woman's faith teach you about trusting God?
3. Write a prayer asking God for healing—physically, emotionally, or spiritually—and trust Him to work in His way.

___

___

___

___

___

CHAPTER 7

THE DIVINE PROMISES OF JOHN 14

Jesus didn't make empty promises. Every word He spoke in John 14 is a foundation for our faith, a constant reminder of who He is and what He does. These promises—peace, guidance, and the hope of eternity—aren't just words. They're living truths that shape our lives when we lean into them.

I've seen these promises come to life over and over again, especially in times when I didn't have the strength to carry myself. Let me share with you how His peace, His Spirit, and His eternal hope have shaped my walk with Him.

HIS PEACE IN THE CHAOS

"Peace I leave with you; my peace I give you. I do not give to you as the world gives. Do not let your hearts be troubled and do not be afraid" (John 14:27).

Not long ago, chaos was my reality. My family was gone. My name was under attack. I was facing legal battles and relentless threats. It was a pressure cooker of fear, anger, and uncertainty. By all accounts, I should have been crumbling under the weight of it all.

But in the middle of that storm, I felt something I couldn't explain—peace. Not the kind of peace that comes from everything being fine—because it wasn't. This was supernatural peace, the kind only Jesus can give. It wasn't tied to my circumstances; it was tied to Him.

That peace didn't fix my problems, but it anchored me. It gave me the clarity to keep moving forward when everything else screamed for me to stop. It reminded me that no matter what happened, He was still in control. That's what His peace does—it silences the chaos and points you back to Him.

The Spirit's Guidance Opens the Door for Miracles

"And I will ask the Father, and he will give you another advocate to help you and be with you forever—the Spirit of truth" (John 14:16–17).

When you're grounded in His peace, you can hear His voice more clearly. That's what happened one day when Mistie and I were out driving through the community. We didn't have a destination in mind. We were just open, asking the Lord to show us who needed Him that day.

That's when He led us to Sara. I told you her story in the last chapter.

Sara was sick—her kidneys were failing, and she didn't have much hope left. But despite her circumstances, she still believed that Jesus could heal her. The Spirit guided us to her home that day, and what happened next was incredible. Mistie prayed boldly over her, declaring healing in the name of Jesus Christ. Not long after, Sara's kidneys were fully restored, defying all medical explanations.

That moment wasn't just about a miraculous healing. It was about the Spirit leading us exactly where we needed to be at exactly the right time. When you follow His guidance, you'll find yourself in places where His promises come alive—not just for you, but for others.

Loving His Children Through the Spirit

One thing I've learned through moments like that is this: the Spirit doesn't just guide us to heal; He guides us to love. There are so many people in the world who feel unseen, unheard, and unloved. And when we follow His prompting, we become vessels of His love for those who need it most.

Sometimes it's a prayer. Sometimes it's a conversation. Sometimes it's just sitting with someone and letting them know they're not alone. The Spirit empowers us to meet people where they are, not with our strength, but with His. Every time I've followed His lead, I've seen lives change—not because of me, but because of Him.

The Eternal Hope of His Promises

"My Father's house has many rooms; if that were not so, would I have told you that I am going there to prepare a place for you? And if I go and prepare a place for you, I will come back and take you to be with me that you also may be where I am" (John 14:2–3).

Here's the ultimate promise: Jesus is coming back. He's preparing a place for us, a place where every wound will be healed, every tear wiped away, and every wrong made right. That promise fuels my hope every single day. It's the hope I carry for my brother Jimmy, knowing I'll see him again. It's the hope that keeps me moving forward, no matter how heavy life gets.

This world is temporary, but His promises are eternal. And because of them, we can face anything.

Reflection Prompt

1. How has Jesus' peace carried you through chaos? If you haven't experienced it yet, ask Him to fill your heart with His peace today.
2. Reflect on a time when the Holy Spirit led you to someone in need. How did it impact both of you?
3. Take a moment to thank Jesus for the promise of eternity. How does this hope change the way you live today?

CHAPTER 8

SPIRITUAL WARFARE

Let's stop pretending that life is just about what we can see. There's more going on than meets the eye. Behind every struggle, every fear, every moment of despair, there's a battle raging—a spiritual battle. And let me tell you, the enemy doesn't play fair. He's strategic. He's relentless. He'll use your past, your pain, and your weaknesses against you. But here's the truth: he's already defeated. The only power he has is what we let him have. And when you know who you are in Christ, you realize you don't have to let him win.

THE ENEMY'S PLAYGROUND: YOUR MIND

The enemy doesn't need to attack your body to destroy you—he just needs access to your mind. If he can twist your perception, manipulate your emotions, and feed you lies, he's got you right where he wants you.

For years, I didn't realize this. I thought my struggles with fear, anxiety, and anger were just part of who I was—something I had to live with. But the truth was, the enemy had been using my past to keep me trapped in a cycle of misery. He'd whisper lies like, *"You're not enough. You'll always be abandoned. No one really cares about you."* And because of my trauma and programming, I believed him.

Let me tell you about a journal entry I wrote in 2017:

"The Lord has revealed to me that I suffer from anxiety because of my fear of abandonment. When I go above and beyond for others and it's not reciprocated in the way I want, I get anxious. That anxiety clouds my perception, makes me misinterpret intentions, and causes me to act out. This fear feeds a cycle of insecurity and pain."

That was me, day in and day out. The enemy had me on a loop, replaying the same fears and insecurities over and over again. Every time I felt abandoned, I'd spiral into anxiety and anger. My mind wasn't a battleground—it was the enemy's playground.

The Turning Point: Reprogramming My Mind

The moment I realized what was happening, everything changed. I saw that my fear, my anxiety, my anger—they weren't just emotions. They were weapons the enemy was using against me. And if I wanted to win, I had to stop fighting in my own strength and start fighting with the tools God had given me.

Here's what I learned: the battle is fought in your mind, but it's won in your spirit. You can't outthink the enemy, but you can outfight him by leaning into the power of Christ.

I started by identifying my triggers—those moments when the enemy would use my past to provoke me. And let me tell you, that was a process. It took prayer, reflection, and a whole lot of humility to admit where I was weak. But once I knew what my triggers were, I started to fight back.

Every morning, I'd meditate for at least 20 minutes. I'd focus on my breathing, clear my mind, and invite God into that space. When I felt darkness or heaviness, I didn't just ignore it. I'd say, *"In the name of Jesus Christ, I command the darkness to depart. Lord, fill me with Your light."*

And it worked. Every single time. The enemy doesn't stand a chance against the name of Jesus. When I stood firm in His truth, the lies couldn't stick. When I invited His light, the darkness had to flee.

Equipped for Battle: The Armor of God

Here's the deal: spiritual warfare isn't just about reacting to attacks. It's about being prepared. God didn't leave us defenseless—He gave us armor. And if you're not putting it on daily, you're walking into battle unarmed.

Here's how the armor of God plays out in real life:

1. **The Belt of Truth**: The enemy is a liar, plain and simple. His whole strategy is built on deception. The only way to fight back is to stand in the truth of who God says you are: loved, chosen, redeemed. When you know the truth, the lies lose their power.
2. **The Breastplate of Righteousness**: This isn't about being perfect—it's about walking in His righteousness. It protects your heart from the enemy's accusations and reminds you that you're covered by His grace.
3. **The Shoes of Peace**: Wherever you go, you carry the gospel of peace. When you know you're saved, loved, and cherished, it changes the way you walk. You bring peace into the chaos, not because of who you are, but because of who He is.
4. **The Shield of Faith**: This isn't just for defense—it's for advancing. The enemy's going to throw darts at you—fear, doubt, temptation—but your faith blocks them. And when you're ready, you can use that shield to charge ahead, knowing you're protected.

5. **The Helmet of Salvation**: This covers your mind. It's your reminder that you're saved, secure, and untouchable in Christ. When the enemy tries to mess with your thoughts, the helmet protects you from his lies.
6. **The Sword of the Spirit**: This is your weapon. It's the Word of God—not just the written Word, but His Word written on your heart. Your testimony is a weapon. Every time you declare what God has done for you, you're cutting through the enemy's lies and taking ground for the kingdom.

Winning the Battle

Here's the truth: the enemy can't win. Don't believe his lies. He can whisper, manipulate, and provoke, but he has no real power over you. The victory has already been won. Jesus sealed it when He broke the bands of death and walked out of the tomb, and when you walk in His authority, you're unstoppable.

But you have to fight. You have to recognize the enemy's tactics and stand your ground. You have to put on the armor of God and walk in the truth of who you are. This isn't a game—it's a war. But when you fight with the power of Christ, you're fighting from victory, not for it.

Reflection Prompt

1. What lies has the enemy used against you? How can you replace them with God's truth?
2. Are you actively putting on the armor of God every day? Which piece do you need to focus on right now?
3. Reflect on a time when you felt the Lord's presence in the middle of a spiritual battle. How did He equip you to stand firm?

CHAPTER 9

EMBERS OF ENDURANCE

Endurance isn't just about survival—it's about transformation. It's about walking willingly into the fire, knowing that God is using it to strip away what doesn't belong and reveal who you were always meant to be. It's about laying everything on the altar and trusting that what He gives you in return will be infinitely greater.

A few years ago, the Lord invited me into the wilderness. It wasn't a command. It wasn't coercion. It was an invitation—a gentle call to leave everything behind and follow Him. At first, it sounded like an adventure, a spiritual journey filled with revelation and divine encounters. And yes, there were moments like that. But what I didn't realize was that the wilderness wasn't just about following—it was about surrender.

THE ALTAR OF SACRIFICE

When I said yes to the Lord's invitation, I thought I understood what I was signing up for. I thought I was already living a life of faith. But the wilderness has a way of revealing things you didn't even know were holding you back. Layer by layer, the Lord began asking me to lay things on the altar—things I didn't even realize I was putting before Him.

My family. My church callings. My temple recommend. My reputation. My job. My friendships. One by one, I had to let them go. Not because they were bad, but because I had allowed them to take priority over my relationship with Him. They had become idols in my life, holding power over me in ways I hadn't realized.

When we consider the history of Israel—from the Bible to the Book of Mormon—we see this pattern repeated over and over. The people of God grow and prosper because of His blessings, but then they become proud. They start putting other things before YHVH. And that pride opens the door to greed, selfishness, contention, and division. The result? Suffering. Every time. But the Lord's love never wavers. He continues to invite us back to Him, to lay everything down and return to the simplicity of dependence on Him.

That's what the wilderness was for me—a season of stripping away. Layer by layer, everything that held power over me was burned away. And what remained was someone I hadn't fully known before: a spiritual giant, fully dependent on the Lord.

THE FIRE OF REFINEMENT

Here's the truth: walking with the Lord through the wilderness isn't easy. It's hard to let go. It's hard to trust. And it's hard to face the fire. But the fire isn't there to destroy you—it's there to refine you. It's there to burn away the dross and reveal the gold.

In Mosiah 3:19, we're taught that the natural man is an enemy to God. But the verse doesn't end there. It says the natural man can be overcome *"if he yields to the enticings of the Holy Spirit, and putteth off the natural man and becometh a saint through the atonement of Christ the Lord."* That's where the transformation happens—in the yielding, the surrender, the submission.

When we willingly submit to the fire, something incredible happens. We become tempered, like steel forged in the heat. Our faith grows stronger. Our patience deepens. Our capacity to endure expands. And with each baptism of fire, we are prepared to withstand even greater challenges.

Lehi taught his children that there is opposition in all things. I've come to know this as absolute truth. With every increase in light, there is an equal and opposite increase in darkness. The more we grow, the more the adversary tries to pull us back. But here's the beauty of it: the fire doesn't consume us. It purifies us. It makes us stronger.

WALKING IN CONFIDENCE

One of the greatest lessons I learned in the wilderness has been this: when we offer everything to the Lord, we gain an unshakable confidence that our course is acceptable before Him. And when you know you're walking in His will, nothing can shake you. Not the opposition, not the trials, not even the fire. You walk with peace, knowing that you're exactly where He wants you to be.

Hebrews 10:34 says, *"You joyfully accepted the confiscation of your property, because you knew that you yourselves had better and lasting possessions."* That's the kind of confidence sacrifice brings. It's not just belief—it's knowledge. It's the assurance that everything you've laid on the altar is safe in His hands, and what He gives you in return is eternal.

The Power of Submission

Here's the truth: the Lord doesn't just want good people. He wants willing hands, broken hearts, and contrite spirits. He doesn't force us into submission—He invites us. And when we say yes, that's where the magic happens. That's where we experience His grace, His power, and His transformation.

The lecture on the law of sacrifice says it perfectly: *"A religion that does not require the sacrifice of all things never has power sufficient to produce the faith necessary unto life and salvation."* Faith isn't built in comfort. It's built in the fire. It's built in the moments when we choose to trust Him over everything else.

Endurance as Transformation

James 1:2–4 says, *"Consider it pure joy, my brothers and sisters, whenever you face trials of many kinds, because you know that the testing of your faith produces perseverance. Let perseverance finish its work so that you may be mature and complete, not lacking anything."*

Endurance isn't just about getting through the hard times—it's about being transformed by them. It's about letting God use the wilderness to shape you, refine you, and prepare you for what's next. It's about becoming a saint, one step at a time, as you walk with Him through the fire.

Encouragement for Your Wilderness

If you're in the wilderness right now, I want you to know this: You're not alone. The Lord is with you every step of the way. The fire you're walking through isn't meant to destroy you—it's meant to refine you. Trust Him. Submit to His process. And hold onto His promises.

Reflection Prompt

1. What is the Lord asking you to lay on the altar in this season?
2. How has God refined you through past trials?
3. Take time to pray and reflect on how you can trust Him more deeply in your current wilderness.

CHAPTER 10

BEAUTY BORN FROM CHAOS

Let's talk about volcanoes. When one erupts, it's pure destruction. The lava doesn't just leave a mark—it wipes everything out. Trees, homes, and entire landscapes are reduced to ash. For a while, it looks like nothing good could ever come from it. But if you come back years later, you'll see something incredible. The ground that was scorched and barren is now bursting with life. The ash has turned into rich soil, and the land is more fertile than ever.

What looked like the end was actually the beginning of something beautiful.

That's how God works. He takes the chaos—the destruction, the pain, the loss—and turns it into something new. It doesn't happen overnight, and it's not always easy to see when you're in the middle of it. But over time, He reveals what He was doing all along: creating beauty from the ashes.

JIMMY'S DEATH: A BEAUTIFUL TRAGEDY

When my brother Jimmy was murdered, it felt like the end of everything. The grief was overwhelming, the kind that doesn't just hit you—it consumes you. For a long time, I couldn't see anything beyond the pain. I couldn't imagine how God could ever bring something good out of something so horrific.

But as the years passed, something began to shift. The pain didn't disappear, but it became... different. It became something sacred. Jimmy's death, as tragic as it was, became the catalyst for my spiritual awakening. It was through that pain that I began to hear God's voice, to see His hand in my life, and to understand His love for me.

Jimmy's life was the seed God used to wake me up. His death caused intense sorrow, but it also planted something beautiful in me. I wouldn't be the man I am today without that experience. And while I still miss him every day, I know he's in the presence of the Lord. That knowledge doesn't erase the pain, but it brings a peace that surpasses understanding.

THE STRIPPING AWAY: LESSONS FROM THE WILDERNESS

Then came 2021—a year that felt like one long volcanic eruption. Leah, my ex-wife, left me. She took our kids, Ellie, Lillie, and Elijah. My reputation was destroyed. Everything I thought I had built was stripped away. I was left standing in the ashes of a life I no longer recognized.

It was the hardest thing I've ever endured. And yet, it was exactly what I needed.

When Leah left, it wasn't just my family that I lost. It was my identity. I had spent so much of my life chasing after things—my role as a father, my callings in the church, my reputation in the community—and I didn't realize how much those things had become idols. They weren't bad in themselves, but they had taken priority over my relationship with the Lord.

The wilderness was the place where all of that was burned away. Layer by layer, God asked me to lay it all on the altar. And as I did, I began to see something I had missed before: I hadn't been chasing after Jesus the way I had been chasing after everything else. My priorities were out of order, and the wilderness forced me to confront that.

The stripping away was painful, but it was also liberating. As each layer burned away, I felt lighter. Freer. More dependent on God. And in that dependence, I found strength I didn't know I had. The wilderness wasn't about losing everything—it was about gaining something greater: intimacy with the Savior.

The Fruit of Suffering

The Apostle Paul wrote, *"We also glory in our sufferings, because we know that suffering produces perseverance; perseverance, character; and character, hope"* (Romans 5:3–4). That's the fruit of suffering: perseverance, character, and hope. It's not something you can manufacture. It's something that's birthed through the fire.

Victor Frankl, a Holocaust survivor, said it another way in *Man's Search for Meaning*: *"When we are no longer able to change a situation, we are challenged to change ourselves."* That's what I learned in the wilderness. I couldn't change my circumstances, but I could change how I responded to them. I could let the fire refine me instead of destroying me.

Through every trial, I've learned to lean into the Lord. To trust Him with the things I can't control. To find peace in His presence, even when everything around me feels like chaos. That peace—the kind that makes no sense to the world—is the fruit of suffering. It's the beauty that's birthed from the ashes.

Perfect Peace

In the middle of the storm, I found something I never expected: perfect peace. Not the kind of peace that comes from everything being fine. This was the peace Jesus had when He was asleep in the boat during the storm, the peace that calmed the waves when His disciples were losing their minds.

There were days when I was surrounded by chaos—legal battles, threats, accusations—but inside, I was calm. I would close my eyes, take a deep breath, and go into the presence of the Savior. I'd visualize sitting with Him, talking to Him, laughing with Him. And in that place, the storm didn't matter. The chaos didn't matter. Because He was with me.

Paul said, *"I have learned the secret of being content in any and every situation"* (Philippians 4:12). That secret is Jesus. It's knowing that no matter what happens, you're in His hands. And when you have that assurance, you can face anything.

THE GIFT OF TRUST

Looking back now, I see how the Lord used every trial to teach me to trust Him. I trust Him with Jimmy. I trust Him with Leah and our kids. I trust that He has them exactly where He wants them, that He's leading, guiding, and protecting them just as He's always done for me. That trust didn't come easily—it was forged in the fire. But it's the greatest gift He's given me.

When we trust God completely, we see beauty in all things. We rejoice in all things. Because we know that nothing is wasted in His hands.

LESSONS FROM THE VOLCANO

The volcano teaches us that destruction is never the end of the story. What looks like devastation is actually preparation. The ashes become fertile ground. The chaos becomes beauty. And the pain becomes purpose.

If you're standing in the ashes right now, I want you to hear this: God is working. It might not feel like it. It might not look like it. But He's there, turning your pain into something beautiful. Trust Him. Lean into Him. And watch what He does.

Reflection Prompt

1. Reflect on a time when God brought beauty out of chaos in your life. How did it shape your faith?
2. Are there areas of your life where you're struggling to see His hand? Pray and ask Him to reveal how He's working.
3. Take time to thank Him for the ways He's transformed your pain into purpose and beauty.

____

____

____

____

____

____

____

____

____

____

____

CHAPTER 11:

IRREVOCABLE BLESSINGS

For the longest time, I thought I understood God's promises. I thought His blessings were contingent on me being "good enough." I thought every mistake I made knocked me back to square one, stuck in a never-ending cycle of striving and falling short. But let me tell you something that changed everything: *His blessings are not about me—they're about Him.* His promises aren't conditional. They're irrevocable because they come from His character, not my performance.

Here's the thing: none of us are worthy. Not one of us. The Bible doesn't sugarcoat it: *"All have sinned and fall short of the glory of God"* (Romans 3:23). It's not about being good enough—it's about His grace. And when you really grasp that, it changes everything. You stop striving and start trusting. You stop carrying guilt and shame and start walking in freedom.

THE WEIGHT OF GUILT AND SHAME

For years, I carried chains I didn't need to carry. Guilt. Shame. The weight of feeling like I had to prove my worth to God, to others, even to myself. Every mistake felt like confirmation of my unworthiness, and I couldn't shake the feeling that I'd never measure up.

In February 2016, something changed. I was praying—pouring my heart out to God—and I heard His voice so clearly. He said:

"Draw near unto Me, My son. When you seek Me, you will find Me. You are free. You are forgiven. Do not be deceived by the shackles of guilt and shame. You are Mine. I have purchased you. And you are clean before Me."

Let me tell you, that moment wrecked me. I'd been carrying guilt and shame like they were mine to bear, but He had already broken those chains. And here's the crazy part: even after that, I still found myself putting them back on. Over and over, He's had to remind me: *"Stop putting those chains back on. You're free."*

That's what guilt and shame do. They convince you that you're still a prisoner, even after the door has been unlocked. But the Lord's been teaching me to live like the free man I am—to stop striving for something that's already mine.

Blessings No One Can Take Away

In 2021, the Lord invited me into the wilderness. At first, I thought I was walking away from everything—my covenants, my blessings, my calling. I wrestled with it. People called me names: cult leader, false prophet, Satan worshipper. And for a moment, I started to believe them. I thought, *"Am I forsaking everything I've worked for?"*

But then the Lord reminded me: *"What I give, no man can take away. What I seal, no man can unseal."* Revelation 3:7 says, *"I am He who opens the door that no man can shut, and closes the door that no man can open."* His blessings aren't tied to religious systems or human approval. They're tied to Him.

The wilderness wasn't about losing everything. It was about learning to trust Him completely. It was about realizing that my identity, my blessings, and my purpose don't come from people—they come from the God who called me.

UNDERSTANDING GRACE

Paul puts it best in Romans 7. He talks about the war raging in his members, how he wants to do good but keeps falling short. He calls himself a wretched man, and honestly, I relate to that. But then he drops this truth in Romans 8: *"There is now no condemnation for those who are in Christ Jesus."*

Think about that: no condemnation. None. Not for Paul. Not for me. Not for you. And then he takes it a step further: *"For I am convinced that neither death nor life, neither angels nor demons, neither the present nor the future, nor any powers... will be able to separate us from the love of God that is in Christ Jesus our Lord"* (Romans 8:38–39).

Let that sink in. Nothing—*nothing*—can separate us from His love. Not your mistakes. Not your failures. Not what other people think of you. His love is unshakable, and His blessings are unchanging. That's grace. And grace isn't just something you experience—it's something that transforms you.

THE ALABASTER JAR

One of my favorite stories in the Bible is about the woman with the alabaster jar. She comes into Simon the Pharisee's house, uninvited, and pours expensive oil on Jesus' feet. She bathes them with her tears and dries them with her hair. And Simon? He's judging her the whole time. But Jesus shuts him down with a story about two people who owed money. One owed a little, the other a lot. Both debts were forgiven. Then He asks, *"Which of them will love him more?"*

Simon says, *"The one who had the bigger debt forgiven."* And Jesus responds, *"Her many sins have been forgiven—as her great love has shown. But whoever has been forgiven little loves little"* (Luke 7:41–47).

That's me. I've been forgiven much, so I love much. I know what it's like to feel unworthy. I know what it's like to carry the weight of guilt and shame. But I also know what it's like to have Jesus take that weight off my shoulders and say, *"You're free. You're forgiven. You're Mine."*

Walking in Freedom

Here's the truth: His blessings are irrevocable. His promises stand firm. And His grace is greater than anything you've done or will ever do. While we might face consequences for our choices in this life, those consequences don't erase His love. They don't undo His promises. The debt has already been paid. We're the ones who keep trying to bring up the charges, but He's already dismissed the case.

When you really understand that, it changes the way you live. You stop striving for approval and start living in freedom. You stop doubting His promises and start standing on them. You realize that nothing—no mistake, no failure, no circumstance—can separate you from His love.

Reflection Prompt

1. Where in your life are you still striving to "earn" God's blessings? How can you release that mindset?
2. Reflect on a time when you experienced His grace in a powerful way. How did it change you?

3. Take time to thank Him for His irrevocable promises. Write a prayer of gratitude for His love and faithfulness.

SECTION 3

LIVING IN FLAWLESS LOVE

CHAPTER 12

THE ESSENCE OF LOVE

Love. It's the heartbeat of the gospel, the foundation of God's character, and the essence of everything we're called to be. Not just any love—*agape* love. The kind of love that flows unconditionally, without strings, without limits. It's not just a feeling. It's a choice, a way of living, a reflection of Christ Himself.

Paul captured it perfectly in 1 Corinthians 13. He wasn't just writing a poetic ode to love; he was laying out a blueprint for what it means to live like Christ. And here's the truth: without love, nothing else matters. Your gifts, your faith, your knowledge—none of it means a thing if it's not rooted in love.

LOVE AS THE FOUNDATION

Paul doesn't hold back: *"If I speak in the tongues of men or of angels, but do not have love, I am only a resounding gong or a clanging cymbal"* (1 Corinthians 13:1). You can have the most beautiful, eloquent words, but if they're not spoken from a place of love, they're just noise. Loud. Annoying. Empty.

And it doesn't stop there: *"If I have the gift of prophecy and can fathom all mysteries and all knowledge, and if I have a faith that can move mountains, but do not have love, I am nothing"* (1 Corinthians 13:2). Imagine that. You could have all the spiritual power in the world—insight, miracles, faith—but without love, it amounts to nothing. Why? Because love is the currency of the kingdom. It's the measure by which everything else is weighed.

Moroni echoed this in Moroni 7, teaching that charity—*agape* love—is the pure love of Christ. He tells us that when Christ returns, it's those who are found filled with this love who will abide the day. Love is eternal. It's not a spiritual accessory; it's the core of who we are called to be.

WHAT LOVE LOOKS LIKE

Paul doesn't just tell us what love isn't—he tells us exactly what it is:

"Love is patient, love is kind. It does not envy, it does not boast, it is not proud. It does not dishonor others, it is not self-seeking, it is not easily angered, it keeps no record of wrongs. Love does not delight in evil but rejoices with the truth. It always protects, always trusts, always hopes, always perseveres. Love never fails" (1 Corinthians 13:4–8).

But here's the thing: these aren't just words to memorize or qualities to aspire to. They're the blueprint for how we're meant to live, every single day.

Love is Patient

Let's start with patience. Love suffers long. It endures. It doesn't give up when things get hard. How many times have we wanted to quit—on people, on situations, on ourselves—because the weight felt too heavy? Love keeps going. It endures the hard conversations, the disappointments, the setbacks. And it does it with kindness. That's the key. It's one thing to endure; it's another to do it with grace.

Love Does Not Envy

Envy is the opposite of love. It's rooted in lack—the belief that what someone else has means there's less for you. But love operates from abundance. When you're walking in love, you're not looking at what others have and wishing it were yours. You're celebrating them, knowing that God's blessings are big enough for all of us.

Love is Not Arrogant or Rude

True love doesn't puff itself up. It doesn't look down on others or dismiss them because they don't fit into a certain box. How often have we seen religious people act rudely, arrogantly, or selfishly, all in the name of God? That's not love. That's pride dressed up as righteousness.

Love is Not Easily Provoked

This one hits home. It's so easy to be provoked, to take things personally, to react out of anger or frustration. But love chooses peace. It doesn't take offense. And here's the thing: not being easily provoked doesn't mean being a doormat. It means setting boundaries that protect relationships rather than destroy them. It means choosing grace instead of judgment.

Love Rejoices in Truth

Love doesn't delight in evil. It doesn't take joy in someone else's failure or pain. Instead, it rejoices in truth, in goodness, in what builds others up. It bears all things, believes all things, hopes all things, and endures all things. That's the power of love—it doesn't give up. Ever.

Love Never Fails

Paul reminds us that everything else will pass away—prophecies, knowledge, even faith. But love? Love never fails. It's eternal. It's what remains when everything else is stripped away.

In 1 Corinthians 13:10, Paul says, *"But when completeness comes, what is in part disappears."* The Greek word he uses for "completeness" is *teleos*, meaning maturity, wholeness, or perfection. Love is what brings us to maturity. It's what refines us, shapes us, and makes us whole.

Moroni reinforces this when he says those who possess charity will abide the day. It's not about earthly perfection—it's about a heart that's been made complete in Christ, filled with His love and compassion.

The Journey to Love Yourself

Here's the secret: you can't pour from an empty cup. To love others, you have to love yourself. And to love yourself, you have to know the love of God. That's been my journey—asking the Lord to help me see myself as He sees me, to love myself with the same grace and compassion He extends to me.

Loving yourself doesn't mean ignoring your flaws. It means embracing the truth that you are loved, cherished, and forgiven—not because of what you've done, but because of who He is. When you see yourself through His eyes, it changes everything. And when you love yourself with His grace, you can love others in the same way.

Choosing Love Every Day

Love isn't a feeling. It's a choice. Every single day, we're faced with opportunities to choose love over judgment, patience over frustration, compassion over indifference. It's not always easy, but it's always worth it.

Consider Jesus. When He hung on the cross, beaten, mocked, and abandoned, He chose love. He said, *"Father, forgive them, for they do not know what they are doing"* (Luke 23:34).

That's the kind of love we're called to—a love that forgives, that endures, that transforms.

Reflection Prompt

1. Reflect on 1 Corinthians 13. Which attribute of love do you struggle with most? How can you grow in that area?
2. Have you asked the Lord to help you see yourself as He sees you? Spend time in prayer, inviting Him to show you His love for you.
3. Think of one way you can intentionally choose love today—in a relationship, a situation, or even toward yourself.

____

____

____

____

____

____

____

____

____

____

____

CHAPTER 13

THE POWER OF GRATITUDE AND LOVE

Gratitude isn't just a nice idea—it's a game changer. It's not something you do when life is good or when you're in the mood. Gratitude is a weapon, a discipline, and a lifestyle. It shifts your focus, realigns your heart, and opens the door for God's love to flow through you in ways you never imagined. And when you combine gratitude with love—*agape* love—you're unstoppable.

GRATITUDE AS THE KEY TO JOY

There's something powerful about choosing gratitude, especially when it's the last thing you feel like doing. Gratitude is an act of defiance against negativity, fear, and despair. It says, *"No matter what's happening around me, I will choose to see God's goodness."*

I remember sitting in a jail cell, completely broken. I had lost everything—my family, my reputation, my freedom. If there was ever a time to wallow in self-pity, that was it. But instead, I made a choice. I started thanking God. It wasn't easy. At first, it felt forced. But as I began to list the things I was grateful for, something shifted.

- I thanked Him for the chance to start over.

- I thanked Him for His presence, even in the darkness.
- I thanked Him for loving me, even when I felt unlovable.

Gratitude didn't change my circumstances—it changed me. It reminded me that even in the worst moments, God was still good. And when I focused on that, I found joy. That's the power of gratitude. It doesn't ignore the pain—it transforms it.

Gratitude in Hardships

Paul's words in 1 Thessalonians 5:18 always hit me hard: *"Give thanks in all circumstances; for this is God's will for you in Christ Jesus."* Not *for* all circumstances—*in* all circumstances. That's the distinction that changes everything. Gratitude doesn't mean pretending everything's fine. It means trusting that God is working, even when you can't see it.

During my wilderness journey, gratitude became my anchor. There were days when I felt like I was losing everything, but I chose to thank God anyway. I thanked Him for the lessons He was teaching me, for the strength He was building in me, and for the intimacy I was experiencing with Him. That gratitude kept me grounded. It reminded me that He was in control, even when my life felt out of control.

The Connection Between Gratitude and Love

Gratitude fuels love. When you're thankful, it's impossible not to love. Gratitude opens your heart, softens your edges, and reminds you of the goodness of God. And when you're walking in gratitude, love flows naturally—love for God, love for yourself, and love for others.

Jesus modeled this perfectly. On the night He was betrayed, He gave thanks. Think about that. He knew what was coming—the betrayal, the denial, the cross—and yet He still gave thanks. That kind of gratitude isn't human. It's divine. And it's the foundation of *agape* love.

When you're rooted in gratitude, you see people differently. You stop focusing on their flaws and start seeing them as God sees them. You start to love them, not because they deserve it, but because He loves you.

Loving Those Who Hurt Us

Let's be real: loving people who hurt you is one of the hardest things you'll ever do. But it's also one of the most transformative. Gratitude is the key. When I started thanking God for the lessons I learned through the people who hurt me, it became easier to forgive them. Gratitude shifted my focus from the pain they caused to the growth it produced.

Paul said, *"Love keeps no record of wrongs"* (1 Corinthians 13:5). That's not easy. But when you pair love with gratitude, it becomes possible. Gratitude helps you see that even the hardest relationships have a purpose. It doesn't mean you ignore the hurt or tolerate abuse—it means you choose to let God use it to make you more like Him.

Gratitude and Self-Love

Here's the truth: you can't pour from an empty cup. To love others, you have to love yourself. And to love yourself, you have to know the love of God.

For years, I struggled with self-love. I saw myself as broken, unworthy, and unlovable. But as I began to practice gratitude, something changed. I started thanking God for who He made me to be. I thanked Him for the gifts He gave me, the lessons I learned, and the person I was becoming. And in that gratitude, I found love—love for myself, rooted in His love for me.

When you see yourself through God's eyes, everything changes. You stop beating yourself up for your mistakes and start celebrating the person He's shaping you into. And when you love yourself with His grace, you can't help but love others the same way.

Gratitude as a Weapon

Gratitude isn't just a discipline—it's a weapon. When the enemy tries to flood your mind with negativity, fear, or doubt, gratitude cuts through the noise. It reminds you of who God is, what He's done, and what He's promised.

Whenever I feel overwhelmed, I stop and make a gratitude list. I thank God for everything I can think of:

- The breath in my lungs.
- The people who love me.
- The lessons I've learned through the pain.

And do you know what happens? The heaviness lifts. The lies lose their power. Gratitude disarms the enemy and fills the space with God's peace.

Practical Steps to Cultivate Gratitude

Gratitude doesn't just happen—it's a practice. Here are some ways to make it part of your daily life:

1. **Start Your Day with Gratitude**: Before you do anything else, thank God for three things. It sets the tone for the day and reminds you of His goodness.
2. **Keep a Gratitude Journal**: Write down at least one thing you're thankful for every day. Over time, you'll start to see His hand in places you didn't before.

3. **Thank God in the Hard Times**: This one's tough, but it's powerful. When things go wrong, thank Him for what He's teaching you. It shifts your focus and builds your faith.
4. **Express Gratitude to Others**: Tell the people in your life what you're thankful for. Gratitude strengthens relationships and builds bridges.
5. **Make Gratitude a Prayer**: Spend time each day thanking God for who He is, not just for what He's done. It deepens your relationship with Him and keeps your heart aligned with His.

REFLECTION PROMPT

1. Think of a challenging situation you've faced. How can you practice gratitude for what it taught you?
2. Reflect on how gratitude has deepened your love for God, yourself, or others.
3. Write down three things you're thankful for today and share them with someone.

____

____

____

____

____

____

____

CONCLUSION

THE CALL TO FOLLOW HIM

This is it—the moment where everything comes together. Every story, every truth, every lesson in this book has led you to this: the call to follow Him. To truly follow Jesus means to embrace His love, receive His grace, and walk in His ways. It's not about having it all together. It's about being willing to take His hand and trust Him with your whole heart.

GOD'S LOVE FOR YOU

Let's start here: God loves you. Not the polished version of you. Not the version you present to the world. The real you. The one who's made mistakes, wrestled with doubt, and struggled to get it right. That's the you He died for. That's the you He loves.

Romans 5:8 says it perfectly: *"But God demonstrates His own love for us in this: While we were still sinners, Christ died for us."* While we were still sinners. Think about that. He didn't wait for you to clean yourself up. He didn't wait for you to fix everything. He came for you as you are.

If you've taken nothing else from my story, take this: if God can redeem a wretched man like me, He can redeem anyone. His love is bigger than your past, stronger than your failures, and more powerful than anything you've ever faced. It's not about being good enough—because none of us are. It's about receiving what He's already given: His flawless love.

The Journey of Transformation

Here's the truth about following Christ: it's hard at first, messy in the middle, but oh, it's gorgeous in the end. Transformation isn't instant—it's a process. It's about surrendering your fears, your imperfections, and your plans and allowing Him to refine you.

I've been there. I know what it feels like to cling to guilt and shame, to believe the lies of the enemy that you're not enough. But God's grace is bigger than all of it. His love isn't a bandage—it's a complete overhaul. When you allow Him to work in you, everything changes. You're no longer defined by your mistakes. You're defined by His mercy.

And that's what He wants for you. Not a life free from challenges, but a life full of His presence. A life where His love transforms your pain into purpose, your chaos into peace, and your trials into triumphs.

Becoming a Zion People

Let's talk about Zion. It's not a place for perfect people. It's a place for willing people. People who have received His love, grace, and law and who live them out with humility and faith. Zion is built on hearts that are turned toward Him, toward each other, and toward the work He's called us to do.

The Lord is coming soon. The signs are everywhere. And when He comes, He's not looking for a spotless record. He's looking for a bride—His people—who love Him, trust Him, and are willing to follow Him wherever He leads.

This is where we are: the hard, messy part of history. But it's also the part where God is preparing a people for Himself. Change is hard. Transformation is messy. But the end is beautiful beyond imagination. Are you ready to say yes? To be part of a kingdom that reflects His heart? To love Him, love others, and walk in the hope of His promises?

The Commandments to Love

Jesus made it simple: *"Love the Lord your God with all your heart and with all your soul and with all your mind. This is the first and greatest commandment. And the second is like it: Love your neighbor as yourself"* (Matthew 22:37–39).

That's it. Love God first. Love your neighbor as yourself. And here's the hard truth: to love your neighbor, you have to love yourself. Not in a self-centered way, but in a way that reflects God's love for you. When you see yourself as He sees you, it changes everything. You stop being your own worst critic and start becoming a vessel of His love.

I invite you to ask the Lord to show you how He sees you. Let Him reveal His heart for you. And as you receive that love, let it overflow into every relationship, every interaction, and every part of your life.

The Invitation to Seek Him

So, here's the question: have you truly sought Him? Have you gone all in, stopped holding back, and given Him your whole heart? He's not hiding. He's waiting. *"Seek and you will find; knock and the door will be opened to you"* (Matthew 7:7).

Jesus doesn't just want part of you. He wants all of you—your fears, your dreams, your struggles, your joy. When you seek Him with your whole heart, you'll find Him. And when you find

Him, everything changes. He's not a distant figure. He's a Savior who meets you where you are, embraces you in your mess, and transforms you from the inside out.

Run to Him

What's holding you back? Whatever it is—fear, guilt, doubt—it's not bigger than His love. Lay it down. Let it go. Run to Him. He's waiting, arms wide open, ready to welcome you home. You don't have to fix yourself first. You don't have to clean yourself up. Just come.

Following Him isn't about perfection—it's about willingness. It's about saying, *"Jesus, I'm Yours. Do whatever You want with me."* And when you do, He'll take you places you never dreamed of. He'll turn your pain into purpose, your brokenness into beauty, and your life into a reflection of His glory.

A Prayer to Begin

If you're ready to say yes to Him, pray this:

"Jesus, I want to know You. I'm tired of holding back. I give You my whole heart—my fears, my failures, my dreams, my everything. Teach me to love You with all my heart, to love myself as You love me, and to love others with Your grace. Transform me. Prepare me. Make me a vessel of Your light. I am Yours. In Your name, amen."

Reflection Prompt

1. What's holding you back from fully surrendering to Christ? Take time to pray and ask Him to help you release it.
2. Reflect on how His love has already transformed your life. How can you share that love with others?

3. Spend time in His presence, asking Him to show you the next step in your journey of following Him.

EPILOGUE

FLAWLESS LOVE IN A FLAWED WORLD

As I sit here, reflecting on the journey that led to this book and the truths we've explored together, one thought rises above the rest: *His love never fails*. It's been the thread weaving through every season of my life—the highs, the lows, the moments of triumph, and the ones where I wasn't sure I'd make it.

This book wasn't just written for you—it was written for me, too. Every word is a reminder of God's relentless pursuit of our hearts, His unshakable promises, and His flawless love for flawed people like me and you.

A VISION OF HIS LOVE

I want you to picture something for a moment: a world where His love reigns. A world where broken people, imperfect and scarred, come together as one—bound not by their achievements, but by their surrender. A kingdom where grace flows freely, where mercy is abundant, and where love is the law.

This is the vision of Zion—a people prepared to receive their King. It's not about building a place. It's about becoming a people whose hearts are fully turned to Him. A people who knows they're loved and who let that love transform their lives and the lives of those around them.

Your Role in the Story

The truth is, you're part of this story. God has called you, chosen you, and placed you here for such a time as this. Your story matters. Your voice matters. And your willingness to say yes to Him has the power to change the world—not because of who you are, but because of who He is in you.

You don't have to have it all figured out. You don't have to be perfect. All you need is a willing heart and the courage to take the next step. Because when you do, His love will do the rest. It will heal you, strengthen you, and flow through you to bring hope and light to a world that desperately needs Him.

The Invitation Continues

If there's one thing I hope you take away from this book, it's this: God's love is for you. It's not just for the polished, the religious, or the people who seem to have it all together. It's for the broken, the messy, the doubters, and the ones who think they've gone too far. His love is for all of us. And it's flawless.

The journey of following Him is just beginning. Keep seeking Him. Keep loving Him. Keep walking in His grace. And as you do, watch what He will do in your life. Watch how He turns your pain into purpose, your trials into triumphs, and your story into a testimony of His love.

A Final Prayer

As we close, let me pray over you:

"Lord, I thank You for the person holding this book. I thank You for their story, their journey, and the way You're working in their life. I pray that they would know Your love in a deeper way than ever before. Show them who You are. Show them who they are in You. Fill them with Your Spirit, and guide them as they follow You.

Transform their hearts, their lives, and their futures. In Jesus' name, amen."

A Journey Worth Taking

This isn't goodbye. This is the beginning of something beautiful. The journey ahead won't always be easy, but it will always be worth it. Keep seeking, keep trusting, and keep walking in the flawless love of the One who gave everything for you.

Made in the USA
Coppell, TX
06 November 2025